Alzheimer's
Disease

Expert Review by
Paul R. Solomon, Ph.D.

SUSAN

DUDLEY

GOLD

Crestwood House
Parsippany, New Jersey

H E A L T H ■ W A T C H

Dedicated to my father, Edward E. Dudley, and to all those who cared for him so lovingly

Acknowledgments

With thanks to:

■■■■ Paul R. Solomon, Ph.D., Professor of Psychology and Chair of the Neuroscience Program, Williams College, Williamstown, Massachusetts; and Co-Director of the Memory Disorders Clinic, Southwestern Vermont Medical Center, Burlington, Vermont, for his advice and review of this book.

■■■■ Sybil Riemensnider, President, and Marilyn Paige, Founder and President Emeritus, Alzheimer's Association, Maine Chapter, for their dedication in helping Alzheimer's patients and their families.

■■■■ All the families who shared photographs of their loved ones for this book.

Photo Credits

Cover: *l.* Courtesy, The National Institute of Neurological Disorders & Stroke. *m.* John Karapelou/PhotoTake NYC. *r.* Courtesy, National Institutes of Health.
Courtesy, the Born family: 35. Courtesy, the Dudley family: 4, 7. Susan Gold: 34. Courtesy, National Cancer Institute: 41. Courtesy, The National Institute of Neurological Disorders & Stroke: 12, 38. Courtesy, National Institutes of Health: 17, 18. Genevieve Palmer: 37. Courtesy, Parke-Davis, a division of Warner-Lambert: 40.
© Catherine Pouedras/Science Photo Library/Photo Researchers, Inc.: 28; © SIV/Science Source/Photo Researchers, Inc.: 22.

Cover and book design by Lisa Ann Arcuri

362.19
GOL

Published by Crestwood House,
A Division of Simon & Schuster,
299 Jefferson Road, Parsippany, NJ 07054

First Edition
Printed in the United States of America
10 9 8 7 6 5 4 3 2 1

Contents

Edward Dudley
as a young
man in the
Army Air Force

Chapter 1

Meet Ted Dudley

Edward Dudley was one of the smartest boys in his class. He spoke at his high school graduation. When he graduated from college, he was one of the students chosen to address the class. His friends called him Ted.

When Ted was in his mid-60s, he began to have trouble remembering things. As the years went by, he had more and more memory problems.

Today, 10 years later, Ted can't remember how to walk or feed himself. He spends most of his time dozing in a chair at a **nursing home**. Ted is one of 4 million

people in the United States who have
Alzheimer's disease (AD).
The disease slowly kills off brain cells in
its victims. It destroys their memory as well
as their ability to do things. Eventually,
Alzheimer's disease kills those who have it.
It is the fourth leading cause of death in
adults. So far there is no cure.

Always Joking

Ted Dudley's sister, Esther, recalls what
he was like as a child. The feature she
remembers most about Ted was his sense of
humor. He could tell a joke without even
smiling. Sometimes people couldn't tell if
he was really joking. His friends, though,
could tell from the look in his eye that
Ted was at it again. He always kept them
laughing.

When World War II began, Ted joined
the Army Air Force. At that time, the Air
Force was part of the Army. Ted trained at
an Army camp in New Jersey. The officers
taught him to fly a plane. He also learned
how to release the bombs the plane would
carry over enemy lines.

While he was in New Jersey, he wrote letters to his girlfriend, Helyn. The way he
described the commander, the base, the
food, and everything else made her laugh
out loud. He was a wonderful writer. In
October 1944, Ted and Helyn got married.

The war ended the next year.

Ted worked as a bookkeeper and a salesman for a paint store. For years he figured complex tax forms. He also handled his church's finances as a volunteer. Ted enjoyed his time on the road as a salesman. He drove throughout the state selling paint supplies. Hardware store owners greeted him warmly whenever he stopped by. Like his boyhood friends, they enjoyed his sense of humor. He knew all the main roads and most of the back roads in the state.

The Dudley family, from left: Helyn, Jane, Edward (Ted), Mark, and Susan

When he wasn't working, Ted tended a huge garden at his house in the country. He enjoyed spending time with his three children.

"Where am I?"

Ted was 67 when Helyn died of cancer. For a while he lived by himself and seemed to be doing fine. But then he began to do odd things. Although he knew how to cook, he often didn't bother. Soon he lost weight. His daughter would stop by to see how he was doing. On one visit, his grandson opened the refrigerator and found it filled with hot dogs and yogurt. The yogurt was so old it had turned green.

His daughter bought groceries for him at the store. When she dropped them off, Ted began to write a check to pay for the food. He had to ask his daughter how to spell her name. He couldn't remember.

Ted and his family decided it would be best if he lived with his sister, Esther. He moved to her house in the fall of 1987. Ted spent much of his time reading in his room. Sometimes Esther went by his door and saw him sitting on his bed, staring into space. But otherwise he seemed to be doing well. She cooked all his meals, and Ted soon gained back the weight he had lost. His son and daughters were glad that he was no longer alone.

Ted and Esther often visited friends in the neighborhood. On Saturday evenings, they went to church suppers. Sometimes they took short trips to view the ocean or the autumn leaves. Esther usually drove. Ted sometimes took the wheel, but he often forgot which way to turn.

During the winter of 1989, Ted and Esther decided to visit friends in Florida. They stopped at a motel on the way. When they arrived in Florida, they stayed at the homes of three friends. At each new place, Ted woke in the night. "Where am I?" he shouted. One night he couldn't find the bathroom. Esther had to guide him there.

When they returned home, Ted began to act strangely. He argued loudly with Esther. Several times he put a pot on the stove and forgot about it. Esther rushed to turn the stove off when the food started to burn. When she asked Ted about it, he didn't remember putting the pot on the stove. He accused her of blaming him for something she had done.

Ted sensed that something was wrong. But he didn't know what the problem was. He asked his daughter to help him move somewhere closer to her house. Esther told her niece she thought Ted might have Alzheimer's disease.

Chapter 2

What Is Alzheimer's Disease?

A German doctor, Alois Alzheimer, first described a certain disease in 1906. Dr. Alzheimer treated a 51-year-old woman who had trouble remembering things. She also found it hard to think clearly. She became less and less able to function.

Dr. Alzheimer diagnosed her as suffering from a form of **dementia**, a brain disorder. The term comes from the Latin words *de* (away) and *mentia* (mind). People with dementia lose their ability to think. They can't remember things. People suffering from dementia are not crazy.

After his patient died, Dr. Alzheimer looked at her brain. He found that many of the cells had been destroyed. The brain was also filled with tangled threads. Brains of other Alzheimer's victims studied after their deaths show the same damage. Scientists don't yet know what causes the damage to the brain. This form of dementia is called Alzheimer's disease, after Dr. Alzheimer.

More than 250,000 Victims a Year

Each year, more than 250,000 people in the United States are diagnosed with Alzheimer's disease. As the population grows older, more people will get AD. If no cure is found, scientists think that 12 million to 14 million Americans could have the disease by the year 2040.

Ninety percent of those with AD are diagnosed after age 65. The other 10 percent of the victims get Alzheimer's in their 30s, 40s, or 50s. Almost 50 percent of people over 85 have Alzheimer's.

The brain damage caused by Alzheimer's is gradual. Some people die three years after the disease strikes, but others can live as long as 20 years. Eventually they can no longer care for themselves. They have to be fed and bathed. They are confined to bed. Alzheimer's disease is always fatal. But some AD victims die from pneumonia or other diseases before Alzheimer's kills them.

People with AD may first notice that
they forget things. While healthy people
may forget names or where they put their
keys, people with AD may forget who
their family members are or how to use
their keys.

Ted Dudley couldn't figure out how to
start his gas lawn mower. He thought he
needed a plug to attach it to an electric
socket. Diana Friel McGowin, another AD
victim, tells about her memory losses in a
book she was able to write before the disease got too bad. One day she drove
home from her husband's job site and
became lost for four hours. She couldn't
remember any of the streets she had traveled for years.

Like a Dark Tunnel

Actress Angie Dickinson, whose sister Mary Lou has Alzheimer's disease, described the terror of not being able to remember where you are, where you have been, or even who you are. "It's like going down a dark tunnel without a guide," Angie Dickinson said on a recent program on National Public Radio.

People with AD have trouble doing tasks they used to do easily. Ted Dudley had worked for years as a bookkeeper, but when he got AD, he couldn't add the numbers in his checkbook. He could no longer remember where to write down the numbers. His handwriting became less and less clear.

Language becomes a problem for AD victims. They can't understand what people mean when they talk. They have trouble remembering words. Sometimes they will say one word when they mean a completely different word. This condition is called **aphasia**.

AD sufferers often lose things or put them in strange places. When Ted Dudley was living with his sister, he sometimes helped her with the groceries. One day she found the grapes in the freezer. Another time he pulled a sock out of his pocket instead of a handkerchief.

People with AD may ask the same questions over and over. That is because they don't remember asking the question just minutes before. One man came home to find 30 messages on his answering machine. Every one of those messages came from his mother, a woman suffering from AD. Each time she left the same message: "Your father is serving me cold breakfasts. I want a hot breakfast."

Behavior Changes

The damage to the brain can cause changes in the way a person behaves and thinks. Many patients become fearful and anxious. They are afraid that other people are going to hurt them.

Ted Dudley had always been a quiet, gentle man. He rarely raised his voice or became angry. As his disease grew worse, he began hitting those who took care of him. He told his daughter that the caretakers were trying to kill him. When she visited, he pulled her near to him. "Get out of here while you still can," he told her. One day he escaped from the nursing home where he was staying. He climbed over a fence and up a tree. He thought he was a prisoner of war. Five workers at the nursing home had to pull him out of the tree and carry him inside.

The brain disease can also cause patients to **hallucinate**. That means they see things that aren't actually there. During a visit with his daughter, Ted began grabbing at the air. "Don't you see that fish?" he asked. Other times he thought his mother was nearby. She had died eight years earlier.

Ted had been an active man. But at his sister's house, he sat for hours on his bed, staring at nothing or sleeping. Alzheimer's patients lose not only the ability to do tasks they used to do. They also may lose the desire to do anything.

Alzheimer's patients may have trouble walking. The brain damage may affect their balance. Diana Friel McGowin tells how she sometimes felt that the floor swayed beneath her feet. She gripped the wall to avoid falling.

Sometimes AD patients can't identify what they see. They may bump into walls or fall down stairs. They may not recognize a close relative or a friend. This inability is called **agnosia**, from the Latin word meaning "not know."

Because patients lose their memory, they may eat too much or forget to eat at all. They may also eat things that aren't good for them. One woman tells of leaving a chicken out to thaw on the kitchen counter. She returned to find that her husband, an AD sufferer, had eaten the entire chicken raw.

Chapter 3

Alzheimer's Disease and the Brain

In an Alzheimer's victim, something
goes drastically wrong in the brain.
Scientists are studying the brain to try
to find out what goes wrong and why.

The brain is the body's control center.
It regulates everything the body does. In
a healthy person, **neurons**, or nerve cells,
carry signals from the eyes, ears, and
other areas to the brain. The brain
decodes these signals. Then it sends signals of its own to respond to the body's
needs. These signals travel along a system
of nerves. If your eyes see that a growling
dog is heading your way, the brain gets

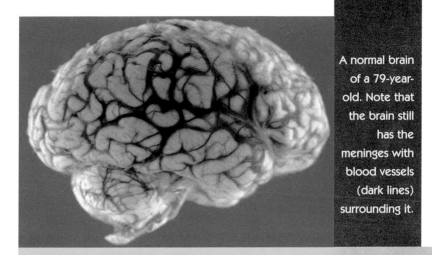

A normal brain of a 79-year-old. Note that the brain still has the meninges with blood vessels (dark lines) surrounding it.

the signal. Then it sends a signal to the legs to run.

The healthy brain also stores past experiences and memories. You may remember that the dog is named Butch and is friendly. Your brain has stored this information. Your response may then be to call to the dog and pat it.

Billions of Nerve Cells

Inside the brain are billions of nerve cells. Each nerve cell has a cell body and wirelike threads. The threads, like rail-road tracks leading from the station, reach out as much as three feet. The nerve cells carry signals to and from the brain along the threadlike railroad tracks. They also contain **proteins**. Proteins are substances found in all living things. They are needed to help cells grow and to repair cells.

Signals pass from one nerve cell to the next with the help of chemicals produced in the brain. These chemicals are called **neurotransmitters**. The nerve cells in the brain use them to communicate with the rest of the body. They are essential for thought, language, speech, emotion, movement, and other functions.

One neurotransmitter, **acetylcholine**, is linked to memory. It is the chemical most affected by the disease. In Alzheimer's patients some of the nerve cells that use acetylcholine are dead or dying. Some Alzheimer's patients have as little as 10 percent of the amount of acetylcholine their brains need to remember things.

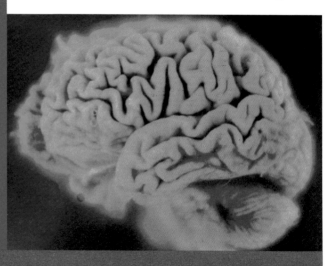

A brain of an 80-year-old with Alzheimer's. The membranes (meninges) surrounding the brain with the blood vessels are missing.

Nerve cells that use other neurotransmitters are also affected. Damage to these cells can cause the AD patient to be moody or unable to do simple tasks or to understand what is being said. The damage can also make the patient angry, hostile, or sad.

In each case, the damaged nerve cells look different from healthy nerve cells. The threadlike tips of the dying nerve cells are tangled. They are also covered with **plaques**—masses of dead nerve endings lumped around pieces of protein. Scientists are trying to find out why the plaques appear and why the cells die.

Chapter 4

Diagnosis of Alzheimer's Disease

So far, there is no simple test for Alzheimer's disease. The only sure way to tell if someone has AD is to examine the brain. This test is usually done only after the patient has died.

Instead, doctors do other tests to see if a patient's unusual or inappropriate behavior results from some other cause. Dementia can be caused by a number of illnesses. Problems with the liver, the thyroid, or the kidney can lead to dementia. Diabetes, a lack of vitamins, or syphilis can also be causes. Some of these conditions can be treated. The patient's dementia may then disappear.

If no other cause can be found, doctors presume the patient has AD. They are right 80 to 90 percent of the time.

In May 1990, Ted Dudley's daughter took him to a doctor for tests. First the doctor asked Ted about his medical history. He told the physician about his family. Neither his mother nor his father had had Alzheimer's disease. But his mother's sister and brother had both suffered from dementia.

The doctor looked at Ted's medical record. He compared his health in the past with the way he was feeling at that moment. Ted's daughter discussed her concerns. She explained how her father visited her and forgot where he was. He also wet his bed. Ted told the doctor he had trouble remembering things.

The doctor weighed Ted. He examined his body. He tested his reflexes and looked into his eyes and ears. He listened to his heart. Ted seemed healthy.

So Many Questions

The doctor asked Ted many questions. Ted told him who he was and where he was. He repeated the doctor's name correctly.

"What is the date?" the doctor asked.

Ted Dudley thought for a moment. "May 21," he said. The real date was May 22.

"What day is it?"

"Tuesday," answered Ted correctly.

A researcher tests an older man for Alzheimer's disease.

"What year is it?"

"1972." He was 18 years off.

The doctor asked him to start with 100 and keep subtracting 7.

"100, 93, 86." Ted began well. He paused. It was becoming harder for him to find the right answer.

"79, 72 . . . ." He could not remember the next number. "I don't know," he told the doctor.

The doctor asked him to describe how to get to his sister's house. Ted had driven that way a hundred times. He started off by naming the right road, but then he became confused. At last he admitted he couldn't remember the way.

Next the doctor said three words and told Ted to remember them. After more questions, the doctor asked him to repeat the three words. Ted remembered only one.

The doctor showed Ted a drawing. It was a design with triangles and squares. He asked Ted to copy it onto a sheet of paper. Ted took his pencil and tried to sketch the design. The shapes were shaky, but they could be identified. The drawing looked like the work of a six-year-old.

Hospital Tests

Ted went to the hospital for more tests. There they tested his blood and urine. He was checked for diseases that might cause his confusion. The wires of a machine were attached to his head with paste. The machine tested to see if his brain waves were normal. This test is called an **electroencephalogram (EEG)**.

The next test was a **CAT scan**. CAT stands for computerized axial tomogram. It takes an X-ray of the brain. The patient is injected with a special dye, which outlines the brain on the X-ray. The X-ray shows if the brain has been damaged by a stroke, by a tumor, or by blood or fluid on the brain.

Ted Dudley lay on his back on a table. The doctor slid the CAT scan machine over the table. Ted's head was placed under the machine, which looked like a giant hair dryer. Ted didn't feel anything when the X-ray was taken.

Other patients may have a spinal tap, in which fluid is withdrawn from the patient's back with a long needle. The fluid is then tested to see if there is an infection in the person's central nervous system.

In some cases, a patient may have an **MRI test**. MRI stands for magnetic resonance imaging. The test gives a detailed view of the brain and spinal cord. From looking at the MRI slides, doctors can tell if a person has had a stroke or other types of brain damage.

The newest test, the **SPECT brain scan**, also views the brain. It can identify atoms in the brain that may indicate that the person has Alzheimer's.

After a long day, Ted and his daughter headed for home. All they could do was to wait for the results of the tests.

Long Journey into Darkness

A few days later, the doctor called. All the hospital tests were negative: no tumor, no diseases, no stroke. In other cases, that would be good news. But in Ted's case, it meant that his confusion was probably caused by Alzheimer's disease. His answers to the doctor's questions and his drawing were also signs that he had AD.

Ted Dudley's long journey into darkness had begun.

Chapter 5

Care and Programs

Some people with Alzheimer's disease can care for themselves for several years. Others need help right away. Sooner or later, all AD victims have to be cared for by someone else. They can no longer live alone.

Often an AD patient is cared for by his or her spouse. Others live with sons or daughters or another member of the family. Seventy percent of the AD patients in the United States are cared for by their families. The remaining 30 percent live in nursing homes or similar places.

After Ted Dudley's diagnosis, his

daughter took him to her house. She had a social worker talk with him to find out if he could live by himself. Some patients also see **occupational therapists**. The therapists test patients to see how much they can do for themselves. They also suggest ways to make life easier and safer for AD patients.

In July 1990 Ted Dudley moved into a home with rooms for elderly people. The home cooked the meals, did the laundry, and arranged special trips for the residents.

For a while, Ted seemed to do all right. He ate with the other residents. He watched TV in his living room. Sometimes he went for walks with his daughter.

But the move had confused him. One night another resident found him standing by her bed. He didn't know how to get to his own room. Another time he fell in his bathroom and couldn't get up. He didn't shave for days at a time. Sometimes he would wear two or three shirts at once.

Residential Homes

After two months, it was clear Ted Dudley needed more help than the home could give. He moved to a different home that offered more care. The new place was known as a **residential care home**. There workers helped him dress. Someone checked on him while he slept to make sure he didn't wander out into the night.

He was very confused when he first moved to the new home. His daughter and the staff at the home tried to help him. They put yellow tape along the stairs leading to his room. Red tape led from his room to the nearby bathroom. That way if Ted got lost, he could follow the tape to his room or to the bathroom.

On his door, his daughter taped a photo of Ted. A sign in big letters said, "Ted's room." She placed other signs throughout his room. "Ted's bed" was taped on the headboard of his bed. On his closet, signs reading "Ted's shirts" and "Ted's pants" told him where to find his clothes.

His daughter also brought a blanket and a chair Ted had used in his own home. That helped him feel more at home.

As Alzheimer's disease destroys more of the brain, patients find it harder and harder to remember things. Many people can recall events that happened when they were young. They may be able to describe a scene from their past, 40 or 50 years ago. But they can't remember where they are at the present time or who is with them. They may stop in the middle of a sentence, unable to recall what they were saying.

Ted Dudley usually remembered his daughter's name. But when his son-in-law visited, he kept asking who he was. Sometimes he called him "Harry." (His name was John.) He also talked about visiting his mother, who had been dead for many years. He laughed as he recalled a day he had spent on his uncle's farm years ago. But he couldn't remember going to the doctor the day before.

Day-Care Centers

Three days a week, Ted Dudley went to a day-care center for adults. Trained staff members worked with the adults. The day began with a reading of the day's newspaper headlines. Then staff members talked about the day's stories. Often the people in Ted's group talked about how things used to be when they were young.

An Alzheimer's patient exercises in a pool.

Each day the group exercised. Sometimes they played with balls outside. On rainy days they did group exercises indoors. Every day was music day. They heard songs from when they were teenagers and young adults. On holidays the group sang special songs. They danced or swayed to the music. Ted could remember the words to most of the Christmas carols and many of the other songs. As soon as the music began, he wore a big smile. Almost everyone in the group enjoyed the music.

The patients also had fun doing craft projects. Ted Dudley liked working with wood the best. He took pieces of wood and glued them together. Sometimes he sanded the wood to make it smooth. As a young man, he had spent many hours in his workshop, sawing lumber and repairing things.

Some of the women worked with yarn. Others pasted pictures in an album. All chose activities they had enjoyed in the past.

Once the group put on a dinner for their families. Each person had a task to do. Ted Dudley cut up the carrots. Others at the center cut the cake for dessert. One person set out the plates. Another put the napkins on the table.

Each task was broken into simple steps. That way, the Alzheimer's patients didn't become confused. Because of the brain damage caused by AD, many patients can do only one thing at a time. What may seem like a simple task to a healthy person may be overwhelming for someone with AD.

Safe Return Program

One day Ted Dudley quietly walked away from the residential home. A police officer found him strolling down a city street. He had no idea where he was or how to get home. He was wearing a bracelet with his name and number. The officer brought him back to the home.

The **Alzheimer's Association** is a national nonprofit group that helps AD patients and their families. It runs a **Safe Return program** to help keep AD patients safe. Each AD patient wears a bracelet that identifies him or her as someone suffering from Alzheimer's disease. The bracelet also carries a telephone number and a code name and number. If an AD patient becomes lost, a police officer or some other helpful person can call the number on the bracelet. By looking up the code number, the Safe Return program can tell who the person is and where he or she lives.

Sometimes a person with AD travels far from home. In one case, a man with AD was missing for two days. He finally called his wife when he remembered his phone number. He was at a bus station in Arizona. The man had traveled alone by bus from his home in Indiana. His wife called the Safe

Return program, which worked with the bus company to bring the man home.

Caring for Patients at Home

A great many AD patients are cared for at home. As the patients become more impaired, caring for them becomes a full-time job. They have to be watched 24 hours a day to make sure they don't hurt themselves. Some patients don't sleep through the night. They may get up in the middle of the night and wander around the house.

Sometimes signs help. A big red stop sign or tape across the door may convince an AD patient not to go into a certain area. Locks may be put on the refrigerator so an AD patient doesn't leave the door open. Knobs can be removed from stoves or a switch put in the back to keep AD patients from burning themselves.

Caring for AD patients takes much patience. They often get frustrated when they can't do things they used to be able to do. It is hard for them to learn new tasks. If they are rushed, tired, or upset, it is even harder for them to do tasks.

Sometimes the patients become very angry. They may try to hit whoever is nearby. They may yell or refuse to move. This behavior is called a **catastrophic reaction**. AD patients don't misbehave on purpose. It is their way of dealing with the confusion, frustration, and fear they experience.

To avoid catastrophic reactions, a caretaker should make each task as easy as possible for the AD patient. It may be very hard for a person suffering from AD to get dressed. He or she may be able to do the tasks one step at a time much more easily. The caretaker can break down the task into simple steps like the following:

1. Put your right foot into your pant leg.
2. Put your left foot into your pant leg.
3. Pull up your pants.
4. Pull up the zipper.
5. Fasten the button.

AD patients may have trouble working zippers or buttons. There are special clothes using Velcro that make it easier for AD patients to dress themselves.

If a person is having a catastrophic reaction, a caretaker must talk in a calm, supportive voice. Sometimes it is best to do the task later, when the person is calmer.

Easing the Losses

As the disease becomes worse, AD patients have to give up many things. Angie Dickinson's sister worked as a typist. As the disease progressed, she began making mistakes in her typing. At night she practiced typing at home. But she just kept getting worse. She finally had to give up her job.

Other AD patients have to sell their

homes, stop driving, let someone else manage their money. Often they lose friends. And, perhaps worst of all, they lose themselves. Eventually, all memory of who they are and what they did in their lives is gone.

People who care for AD patients try to let them do as much as they can for as long as possible. They try to ease the losses AD patients have to endure.

Ted Dudley enjoyed driving, but as his disease got worse, he could no longer drive. His daughter took him for rides. He gave directions and told her how to operate the car. Often the directions and the instructions were wrong. But Ted enjoyed the feeling that he was back in the car again. He kept his car keys in his pocket and often took them out and played with them.

Family members, too, feel losses. They lose a spouse, parent, or grandparent to the disease. Ted Dudley's 17-year-old grandson, Sam, said Alzheimer's has made a complete change in his grandfather. "His personality has totally faded," Sam said of his grandfather. "He can't give me the attention he used to. He can't do anything with me." Sam said seeing his grandfather in the nursing home depresses him "because he is a shell of the person he once was."

In the last stages of the disease, patients can no longer walk. They have to sit in a chair or lie in bed. They become unable to control urine and bowel movements and

must wear diapers. They can no longer feed themselves or recognize loved ones. At that stage most patients go to a nursing home. Some, however, are cared for at home until they die.

Help for the Caretaker

It is said that Alzheimer's disease claims at least two victims: the person who has AD and the person who cares for the patient. It is sad and frustrating to care for a loved one dying from Alzheimer's disease. It is also hard work. Changing an adult's diapers, washing and feeding someone who resists, and always watching can exhaust anyone. When the patient becomes angry, it is difficult to stay calm.

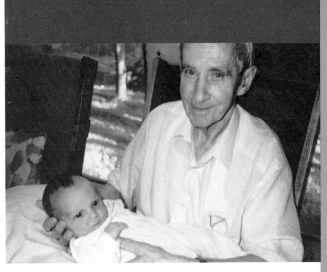

Lack of sleep, hard work, anxiety, and sadness take their toll. Caretakers can become sick if they don't have time to themselves. Alzheimer's Association chapters in many states offer a respite program for caretakers. They send in a trained volunteer who stays with the AD patient while the caretaker takes a break. Caretakers can also bring the AD patient to a day care center for adults. In some cases, though, there are no day care centers nearby or the cost is too high.

The Alzheimer's Association also runs

35

support groups for caretakers, AD patients, and their families and friends. Group members share their feelings and help each other with problems.

Diana McGowin started a group just for AD patients. She and other AD patients meet and talk about what it's like to have AD. Many Alzheimer's patients do not understand that they have the disease. But a few, like McGowin, know too well what is happening to them. "The shared tears, laughter, and hope are a balm to the troubled spirit," she writes in her book. With the help of the Alzheimer's Association, groups now meet in several states.

Nursing Home Care

In November 1990 Ted Dudley moved to a nursing home. His disease had become worse, and the residential care home could no longer care for him. At the nursing home, aides dress and feed him. He spends his day sitting in a chair or lying in bed. He watches movies with other patients, but he can't follow the story. On good days he looks at the family photo album with a staff member or his daughter. Sometimes he throws a ball during the recreation program.

There are weights and a stationary bike for those who can use them. Some patients work on simple puzzles or help care for the nursing home's pet rabbit. On sunny days patients sit outside on the patio and admire the flowers. Patients are encouraged to draw, paint, or work on hobbies. Family members, including children and pets, often stop by to visit.

Bands, singers, and other musicians put on shows at the home. Ted Dudley still smiles when he hears the music.

Some nursing homes have special units for Alzheimer's patients. The doors are equipped with alarms and stop signs. That keeps patients from wandering outside and becoming lost. There are roomy areas where the patients can walk. Many AD patients pace back and forth much of the day.

Lauren Day, 7, visits with her grandfather, Ernest A. Palmer, at the nursing home where he lives. Mr. Palmer was diagnosed with Alzheimer's when he was 62. He is 69 in this photo.

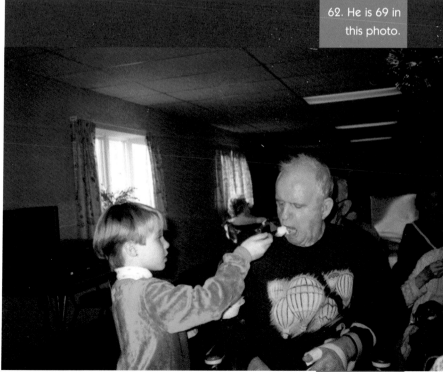

Staff members are trained to work with AD sufferers. They speak in calm voices and don't rush the patients. They try to do activities that interest them. They often talk about the past, since that is one thing many AD patients can remember.

Care is Costly

Caring for AD patients is expensive. It can cost as much as $20,000 a year to take care of an AD patient at home. The cost rises to about $36,000 a year if the person is in a nursing home. Adult day care centers charge between $25 and $45 a day. The price tag for a month's supply of diapers is $100 to $250.

According to the *Wall Street Journal*, Alzheimer's disease costs Americans an estimated $100 billion a year. That figure covers the price of care, treatment, diagnosis, and lost wages of caretakers. Most of that amount is paid by AD victims and their families. About 10 percent is paid by the federal and state governments.

A man with Alzheimer's disease plays the cymbals during a recreation period at a facility for AD patients. Many AD patients enjoy music.

Chapter 6

Treatment
and
Research

Alzheimer's research has a long way to go. Scientists have theories, but they do not yet know for sure what causes the disease. Because they haven't been able to find the cause, they don't know how to prevent Alzheimer's or how to cure patients who have the disease.

But scientists have learned much in the last few years. Their research has led to some breakthroughs in treatment.

Drugs Can Help

On September 9, 1993, the **Food and Drug Administration (FDA)** approved the first medicine for treating AD. The drug, **Cognex**, increases the amount of acetyl-choline in the brain. AD patients don't have enough of this chemical, which is linked to memory.

In a six-month study of the drug, Cognex helped ease the symptoms of AD in 70 percent of the patients taking the highest dose. It helped patients remember, speak, understand, and carry out tasks better than those who weren't taking the drug. Cognex also slowed the effects of Alzheimer's. Some of those on the drug stayed at the same level for six months instead of becoming worse.

So far, Cognex has helped people with mild to moderate cases of AD. Further tests will show whether it can help people with more severe cases. Drug companies are testing similar medications to find treatments that will help other AD victims.

Doctors are also giving some AD patients drugs to help keep their emotions under control. AD patients who are depressed or upset have been helped by a number of medications, called mood-alter-

An employee of Warner-Lambert, makers of Cognex, carefully inspects the capsules as they are packaged.

ing drugs. Studies are under way to find out which drugs can help AD patients the most. Though both Cognex and mood-altering drugs help the symptoms of AD, they do nothing to stop the disease.

A scientist works on an experiment in a laboratory. Researchers studying Alzheimer's are hoping to find a cure for the disease.

Finding the Cause

Scientists are working to find the cause of AD. There are many questions that need answers. Why does Alzheimer's take 65 years or more to affect its victims? Why do some of the nerve cells die while others are not affected?

Some believe a faulty **gene** is responsible. Genes are tiny units within each of our cells that determine our features. We inherit genes from both our mother and father. The genes determine the color of our hair and whether we are tall or short. Genes can also pass along diseases.

People with AD may inherit faulty genes from their parents. More than one gene may cause AD. If researchers can find the genes that cause AD, they may be able to make a drug to replace them.

Dr. Alan Roses and a group of scientists at Duke University believe AD may be caused by the lack of a certain protein in a gene. They found that many of the AD patients they studied were missing a protein called **apo-E3**. Other researchers believe AD may be connected to a problem in a different gene. Scientists are also studying to see if the disease is caused by viruses, poisons, or some unknown factor.

Other researchers are trying to find a **biological marker** in AD patients. A biological marker for AD would be something found only in the bodies of AD patients. If tests showed it was present in the person's body, then doctors would know that that person had the disease. Researchers have studied more than 70 substances they thought might be markers. So far, none have been proven to work as tests for AD.

Researchers may have made a breakthrough, however. In late 1993, scientists developed a skin test that may show that a person has AD. The skin test has not yet been proven. Such a test would save much time and money in trying to diagnose Alzheimer's. It would also tell when patients did not have AD, and they could be treated more quickly for the disease that was causing the symptoms. If the skin test works, doctors will be able to treat AD sufferers earlier. They may be able to delay AD symptoms.

Finding a biological marker may also give clues to the cause of the disease. It may lead doctors to find ways to prevent people from getting Alzheimer's.

Research is also being done to study how AD affects patients' ability to see and recognize objects. With that information, special living areas can be built for AD patients. Activities can also be designed that will be easier for patients to do. Such research can make life easier and less confusing for AD patients.

Researchers are hopeful they will find a cure for AD in the next 10 years. They continue to study Alzheimer's victims for the answers. Researchers depend on volunteers to participate in tests on drugs. They also rely on Alzheimer's patients who donate their brains for study after they die.

In life, Alzheimer's patients must function as best they can with a brain that no longer works properly. In death, their damaged brains may someday offer scientists the key to the mystery of their disease.

    ะ๑   ะ๑   ะ๑   ะ๑   ะ๑

Edward Dudley died March 17, 1995. He donated his body for medical research.

    ะ๑   ะ๑   ะ๑   ะ๑   ะ๑

For Further Reading

Beckelman, Laurie. *The Facts About Alzheimer's Disease.* New York: Crestwood House, 1990.

Berger, Melvin. *Exploring the Mind and Brain.* New York: Crowell, 1983.

Bruun, Ruth Dowling, and Bertel Bruun. *The Brain—What It Is, What It Does.* New York: Greenwillow Books, 1989.

Derby, Pat. *Visiting Miss Pierce.* New York: Farrar, Straus, & Giroux, 1986.

Facklam, Margery, and Howard Facklam. *The Brain: Magnificent Mind Machine.* New York: Harcourt Brace Jovanovich, 1982.

Frank, Julia. *Alzheimer's Disease: The Silent Epidemic.* Minneapolis: Lerner Publications, 1985.

Guthrie, Donna. *Grandpa Doesn't Know It's Me.* New York: Human Sciences Press, 1986.

Klein, Norma. *Going Backwards.* New York: Scholastic, 1986.

Lambert, Mark. *The Brain and Nervous System.* Englewood Cliffs, NJ: Silver Burdett Press, 1988.

Landau, Elaine. *Alzheimer's Disease.* New York: Franklin Watts, 1987.

McGowin, Diana Friel. *Living in the Labyrinth: A Personal Journey Through the Maze of Alzheimer's.* New York: Dell Publishing, 1993.

Martin, Paul D. *Messengers to the Brain: Our Fantastic Five Senses.* Washington, DC: National Geographic Society, 1984.

Silverstein, Alvin, and Virginia Silverstein. *World of the Brain.* New York: William Morrow, 1986.

Whitelaw, Nancy. *A Beautiful Pearl.* Morton Grove, IL: A. Whitman, 1991.

For More Information

Alzheimer's Association
919 North Michigan Avenue, Suite 1000
Chicago, IL 60611-1676
1-800-272-3900
(Look in the telephone book for your local chapter.)

Alzheimer's Disease Education & Referral Center
P.O. Box 8250
Silver Springs, MD 20907-8250
301-495-3311

Alzheimer's Disease Society of Canada
491 Lawrence Avenue, West, #501
Toronto, Ontario, Canada M5M 1C7

Centers for Disease Control
Public Inquiries, Mail Stop A-23
1600 Clifton Road
Atlanta, GA 30333

National Health Information Clearinghouse
P.O. Box 1133
Washington, DC 20013
1-800-336-4797
(in Virginia: 703-522-2590)

National Institutes of Health
9000 Rockville Pike
Bethesda, MD 20892
301-496-4000

Glossary

acetylcholine A chemical in the brain that helps a person to remember things.

agnosia The inability to recognize or identify people or objects.

Alzheimer's Association A national, nonprofit group founded in 1980 to help Alzheimer's victims and their families and to push for research.

Alzheimer's disease (AD) A disease that destroys brain cells. Eventually, Alzheimer's victims lose the ability to think, remember, and function. Alzheimer's disease is fatal.

aphasia The inability to say what you want to say. The problem is caused by brain damage.

apo-E3 A form of protein that is missing in many Alzheimer's victims. Some researchers believe that its absence may lead to Alzheimer's disease in 60 percent of the cases.

biological marker A substance that shows the presence of a disease or condition. For example, sugar in the urine is a sign of diabetes.

catastrophic reaction An AD patient's response to confusion, fear, or frustration. The person may kick, hit, scream, or refuse to move.

CAT scan Computerized axial tomogram. It takes an X-ray of the brain and is used to rule out other causes of dementia.

Cognex A new medicine that helps ease the symptoms of Alzheimer's disease in some patients.

dementia A brain disorder that causes people to lose their ability to think, remember, and function properly.

electroencephalogram (EEG) A procedure that tests brain waves.

Food and Drug Administration (FDA) A government agency that makes sure that prescription medicines are safe and effective.

gene A tiny unit in each cell that determines a person's features.

hallucinate To see things that aren't there.

MRI test Magnetic resonance imaging test. It gives a detailed view of the brain tissue and can show if a person has had a stroke or other types of brain damage.

neuron A nerve cell, a cell that carries messages from parts of the body to the brain or from the brain to parts of the body.

neurotransmitter A chemical that the brain cells use to communicate with each other and with the rest of the body.

nursing home A facility where trained staff members provide complete care for disabled residents. In some cases, residents have to be fed and dressed.

occupational therapist A professional who tests Alzheimer's patients to see what tasks they can do and gives advice on ways to make life easier for the patients.

plaque A mass of dead nerve endings and pieces of protein. It can stick to nerve cells and damage them.

protein A substance needed for cell repair and growth. It is found in all living things.

residential care home A facility with trained staff members where people with Alzheimer's disease and other problems can live and get help with everyday tasks.

Safe Return program A program run by the Alzheimer's Association to help identify lost AD patients. Participants wear bracelets with a telephone number and code name to identify them.

SPECT brain scan A new test that views the atoms in the brain and may be useful in diagnosing Alzheimer's disease.

Index

acetylcholine, 18, 40
agnosia, 15
Alzheimer, Dr. Alois, 10, 11
Alzheimer's Association, 30, 35, 36
aphasia, 13
apo-E3, 42

biological marker, 42, 43
Born, Clyde, 35
brain, 11, 16, 17, 23, 24, 27, 40, 43
brain damage, 11, 14, 15, 23, 29

caretakers, 34, 35
CAT scan, 23
catastrophic reaction, 31, 32
Cognex, 40, 41
costs, 38

Day, Lauren, 37
day-care centers, 28, 38
dementia, 10, 11, 20, 21
Dickinson, Angie, 13, 32
Dudley, Edward (Ted), 4, 5, 6, 7, 8, 9, 12, 13, 14, 15, 21, 22, 23, 24, 26, 27, 28, 29, 30, 33, 34, 36, 37, 43
Dudley, Esther, 6, 8, 9
Dudley, Helyn, 6, 7, 8

electroencephalogram (EEG), 23

Food and Drug Administration (FDA), 39

genes, 41, 42

hallucinations, 14

McGowin, Diana Friel, 12, 15, 36
memory, 6, 12, 15, 18, 27, 33, 40
mood-altering drugs, 41
Morrison, Sam, 33, 34
MRI test, 24

nerve cells, 16, 17, 18, 19
neurons. *See nerve cells.*
neurotransmitters, 18, 19
nursing home, 5, 14, 25, 34, 36, 38

occupational therapists, 26

Palmer, Ernest A., 37
plaques, 19
proteins, 17, 19, 42

residential care, 26, 36
Roses, Dr. Alan, 42

Safe Return program, 30, 31
skin test, 42, 43
SPECT brain scan, 24
spinal tap, 24